PARTY PIECES

PARTY PIECES

By

JULIA CLEMENTS

PEARSON : LONDON

© Julia Clements, 1960

PRINTED IN GREAT BRITAIN BY
MORRISON AND GIBB LIMITED, LONDON AND EDINBURGH

Contents

INTRODUCTION 7

COCKTAILS AND BUFFETS 9

SPECIAL OCCASIONS 31

FORMAL AND INFORMAL 45

FOR TEENAGERS 63

FUN FOR CHILDREN 79

SOMETHING NEW 89

CHRISTMAS 107

HOW TO DO IT 135

CARE OF CUT FLOWERS 139

RECIPES 143

List of Colour Plates

	Facing Page
AN ENGAGEMENT-PARTY BUFFET TABLE	96
MIMOSA AS A DOMINATING PARTY MOTIF	97
A PARTY ARRANGEMENT FOR A SIDEBOARD	112
A CHRISTMAS DINNER PARTY	113

Introduction

*Be not forgetful to entertain strangers, for
thereby some have entertained angels unawares.*

Hebrews xiii, 2

SINCE I wrote my first book, *Fun With Flowers*, great advancement has been
made in the world of flower arrangement. It has become a social grace,
and many thousands of women have found a new interest and outlet
through this expressive art. There is no doubt that as time goes on flowers
are assuming an ever-increasing importance in our lives.

Despite this I find that, as more and more books on entertaining appear,
references to flowers at parties are often either relegated to the back of the
book, or written off with just one page of description. Is this, I wonder,
because they are *expected* to be there, and so need no more qualification for
inclusion in the book ?

This omission has always seemed a pity to me for, while agreeing that food
and drink are important at parties, I would like to see the floral decorations
lifted from the accepted part they so often play and promoted to one of the
star roles—even that of ballerina assoluta !

Some of the most successful parties I have attended or have given have been
planned round the flowers. At such events they certainly have been talked
about, not only because ' they are lovely ' (all flowers are lovely) but because
they have played an important interpretive part in the overall party scheme.

Although I have purposely called this book *Party Pieces*, I must warn you
that it is not specifically on *how* to entertain, nor is it a cookery book. It is
an extension of my reflections on flower arrangement in connection with
parties, written to fill what I think has been a gap, giving hints and ideas on
how flowers can help you to toe the party line ; though I have included a
number of well-tried recipes, gathered on my travels. While not purposely
contriving to be different for the sake of it, I always enjoy introducing novelties
to surprise and delight my guests.

I am often asked if there are any golden rules for party giving, and I find it
very difficult to generalise—so much depends upon the background, the size
of the party and expenditure possible. Personally, I enjoy conversation and

so prefer smaller gatherings where one is able to develop a certain train of thought or a theme started perhaps by a chance remark which can be pursued to a conclusion. But when I organise a larger party I make sure that guests are introduced to each other with a tag or biographical note which will help to open some kind of conversation. It is so easy to introduce Jane Smith ' who has just returned from Rhodesia ' to Patrick Brown ' who is keen on sailing.'

Similarly, I do not care to break up a group or a couple who are obviously getting on well together. If such action is thought necessary an approach can be made with the remark, ' Jane, when you are free I have a friend who is dying to meet you.' If Jane is getting on very well with Mr. Brown she can reply ' Thank you, I'll come in a moment,' and forget it ; if on the other hand she wishes to leave Mr. Brown, she has been given the opportunity to do so.

Of course we all have our pet methods ; but here are a few principles to bear in mind :

> Give a party because you want to.
>
> Introduce guests with something more than just their names.
>
> Don't purposely separate groups ; test to see if it is acceptable.
>
> Make a highlight of your floral decorations ; your skill here can be talked about for weeks afterwards.
>
> Plan your eats and drinks well in advance and on the generous side. Only when you know that all is in order can you relax sufficiently to enjoy *yourself*, which goes a long way towards making you the perfect hostess you know you can be.

I have loved making this book, and hope that it will be of much practical value in stimulating imagination and releasing some of the ideas you probably have stored away. Certainly the basic hints on the care and use of flowers are intended for all, but how you finally display the flowers at your party will depend on yourself. Flower arrangement is an expressive art and the final issue will show *you* as the artist.

JULIA CLEMENTS

Cocktails and Buffets

Cocktails and Buffets

'LET'S give a cocktail party!' How blithely we utter these words, perhaps because we feel that such a party is the easiest way of entertaining a number of friends.

This does not mean that more time and money must necessarily be lavished on the event, but it does mean that careful thought should be given to your plans some time before the actual date of the gathering. Do try to include an original idea, some little 'different' touch, which is all your own.

You could introduce a new drink, one that you have sampled on an off-the-beaten-track holiday. If you possess the background which allows it, try an amusing décor. Perhaps you have gathered some claim to fame for your flower arrangements or cooking; if you have, introduce a special flower scheme and display masses of one kind of flower. Or give your friends the pleasure of experiencing one of your famed buffet dishes. In other words, your party will have a better chance of being a success if you specialise, rather than offer the now-too-familiar cocktails to friends who stand huddled together in a crowded room.

A St. Andrew's Eve party will always prove popular if you are a Scot or have Scottish friends, in whatever part of the world you may find yourself on 30th November. Pine-cones, heather and tartans all form the background to these celebrations. At such a party, instead of the usual cocktail canapés, try offering wee bannocks, oatmeal cakes or biscuits, mealie puddings, or liver sausage; and if some of the guests stay on longer by invitation, a real Scottish Haggis would be welcomed.

As whisky is Scotland's national beverage, why not avoid the usual cocktails and provide instead any drink with whisky as an ingredient? My favourite is a whisky punch; here is the recipe. Place the grated rind of three lemons with ½ lb. castor sugar in the base of a punch bowl, pour over two bottles of whisky and four of water, and add the three lemons, cut in very thin slices. This makes an agreeable cold punch, enough for two good drinks for 20 guests. (Other recipes featuring whisky will be found at the end of the book.)

To ensure that your Scottish party will be the talk of the town, offer each departing guest a small glass of the true Athole Brose. The recipe for this famous drink is said to have been handed over as a gesture of friendship to the Duke of Atholl by Alexander Seton, Lord Gordon (c. 1421). It was formerly referred to in Scotland as Heather Ale, although it is really a liqueur, the taste and effect of which will be greatly enjoyed, specially by those who are sampling it for the first time. Here is the recipe : 1 bottle of whisky (Scotch, of course !), $\frac{3}{4}$ lb. coarse oatmeal, $\frac{3}{4}$ pint thick cream, $\frac{3}{4}$ lb. liquid honey, a few drops of vanilla essence, if liked. Pour the bottle of whisky into a bowl and immerse in it the oatmeal tied in a muslin bag. Cover and leave for twenty-four hours. Squeeze the oatmeal bag into the whisky, making it creamy, and remove. Pour in the cream and add the honey, stirring all the time—the mixture will become very slightly glutinous. Now comes the interesting part—heat a tablespoonful of whisky over a flame until it catches fire and drop this into the mixture, still stirring. This makes the brew thinner.

The drink tastes of oatmeal and whisky, the cream softens what might other-wise be considered a hard drink, and the burning whisky dissolves the honey. A word of warning : guests who partake of this heavenly brew must remember that its potency has been increased by the twenty-four-hour fermenting of the whisky and oatmeal.

Flowers should play an important part as decorations at a cocktail party. In fact, if their use is exaggerated, they can assume a star role. In the early part of the year, try using only Mimosa as your flower scheme. I have done this with great success, but you must use it profusely, displaying masses of it on the mantelshelf, tables and pedestals, so that it becomes the talk of the gathering and is remembered. Order a basket (or more) of Mimosa direct from your florist, and ask for it to be delivered in the basket. If you recut the stems before placing them in very hot water to swell the wood, and then arrange the sprays in warm water to which a little sugar has been added, you will find they will stay fresh and fluffy for quite a long time.

Not only does the colour of this delightful blossom add gaiety to the winter atmosphere : the skip baskets in which the flowers travel to our flower markets from the south of France can be used as containers for your tit-bits and canapés. Fix the lid open with wire, line the basket with greaseproof paper or table napkins on which the canapés are placed, and for extra effect attach a spray of Mimosa to the open lid with perhaps some mauve ribbon.

To carry the idea a little further, serve a Mimosa cocktail. This is really delicious, and if you have not yet tried it you have a pleasure to come. Use one-third Benedictine, one-third Vermouth, and one-third gin, and shake with ice. One bottle of each will make enough for 30 guests, allowing them three drinks each.

Have you tried giving a cocktail party on May Day ? This can prove to be an unusual success if you use Lilies of the Valley as your flower theme. For such a party your drinks could be served from a table completely covered with pale green material, or a sheet tinted pale green with a cold dye, with large bowls of Lilies of the Valley placed around. If these exquisite flowers appear small in scale to your table setting, try placing two tall vases full of greenery, such as juniper or cupressus, in the shape of trees at each end of the serving table and insert between the greenery tubes of water containing the lilies. These tubes can be obtained from chemists, though plastic toothbrush holders or small bottles may be used instead. This idea will give a ' lift ' to these tiny flowers, and you can emphasise their importance by placing smaller bowls of them on lower tables. For further emphasis, the air can be sprayed with Muguet scent or toilet water, or, if your party is in the evening, you might try putting a few spots on the electric-light bulbs ; the heat of the light will release the scent. A favourite trick of mine is to add a few drops of scent to boiling water : the steam perfumes the atmosphere.

Another May Day idea is to introduce a miniature maypole in the centre of your serving table, with different coloured ribbons leading to dishes of sandwiches and canapés. For drinks, nothing could be better than light champagne, although Rhine wine and sparkling Moselles are also an excellent choice. A White Lady cocktail could be served, if preferred ; for this use one part Cointreau, one part lemon juice and two parts gin.

During the month of May, when Tulips abound, they can be massed round the house, some perhaps arranged in lined wooden clogs. When Lilac appears, nothing could be more lovely than to use branches of this sweet-smelling blossom in mauves, pinks and purples, with no other floral additions. I remember visiting Lady Astor at Cliveden once during May, and seeing in one corner of the entrance hall a massed display, rising to about ten feet from the ground, of all shades and varieties of Lilac. I discovered later that the head gardener had placed the stems in a series of tin tubes fixed to a frame in rows one above the other. The effect was quite devastating, but could easily be copied by anyone using this lovely flower massed in vases round the party room.

If guests are to stand, arrange the flowers on tall pedestals, or raised on boxes covered with pink paper or material, placed on the serving table. Lilac can be cut short and arranged at the top of tall candelabra, but however you use it, you may like to emphasise the pink, mauve and purple colour scheme. If your party is at night, try fixing a spotlight to focus on to the Lilac (pinks show up well in artificial light, but purples and mauves are inclined to appear dull unless spotlit). To extend your colour scheme, why not cover the serving table with a pink cloth and serve pink gin or pink champagne, both made pink

● *An attractive setting for a buffet. The flowers
are placed out of the way on plinths
standing behind the table.
Held on pin-holders under wire-netting in
shallow containers, they are arranged
irregularly with the ends flowing out over
each end of the table.*

● Beside the welcome cocktail tray is a dramatic design of
four Anthuriums in a framework of leaves,
arranged on a tray behind an African carving.

● Mimosa adds gaiety to a winter party.   Recut the stems and
place them in hot water for ten minutes before
arranging the sprays in warm water to which has been
added a tablespoonful of sugar.

● *Swerved designs are ideal placed at the side of each end of a*
  serving table.   For such a purpose always use
  a tall container which lifts the flowers away from the food.

● *Onion heads and Fatsia leaves in a green glass bottle decorate*
  an informal curry party buffet table.
  The dishes containing different curries stand on pedestal heaters.

16

● This unusual design
could cause a stir
at a party.
Three Strelitzia
Reginae blooms,
arranged on a
pin-holder behind
a piece of bark wood,
are set on a
large pottery
container filled
up with wood
and moss.
Oranges and violets
repeat the colours
of the flowers.

● *Wine and cheese parties are popular because they are easy to organise and can be held
at any hour and for any number of guests. Grapes are the main feature
of this decoration; the lower bunches are fixed with wire
to the bronze ewer, round which vine leaves are twisted. A small dish in the
opening of the ewer holds stems of coral pink roses and more grapes.*

● *A green colour theme emphasised with glass candlesticks*
and plates, and a large green
lidded dish filled to overflowing with fruit.

● *Heather, pine, cones and teazles are ideally suited for decorating*
a St. Andrew's Eve buffet table.   The plant material,
inserted into a large potato, stands on a
slab of bark, and the candelabrum is swathed with plaid.

21

● *A design for an 'after-fishing' get-together,*
or for a party where fish dishes
predominate . . . Bulrushes, grasses and yellow
Solidago grouped in a fish-creel
placed among netting, glass fishing
floats, shells and 'fishy' pottery.

22

● *Lilies of the Valley massed in a glass*
  sugar basin accentuate
  the May theme of this table setting.

(See p. 136 for details of this design.)

● *A white and pale pink triangular design, in which sprays of*
Deutzia Gracilis and pink Tulips are held by crumpled wire-netting.
Try this on a sideboard or hall table.

24

by the addition of a few drops of Angostura bitters? And how about a Pink Lady cocktail? To make this, you use one part Cointreau, one part lemon juice, two parts gin, adding a few drops of Angostura bitters.

Other pink drinks are Cinzano with soda water and Campari with lemonade; these could be served on pink painted or plastic trays.

Once you begin to think about it, the ideas for specialising are endless. I remember once trying a red theme, using flowers of all tints and shades of red placed about the house and on the serving table. The only relief was given by a frill of apple-green ribbon round a posy of red Carnations, which I set on the curled banister at the foot of the stairs. Flowers of all one colour are sure to be noticed and talked about, and are certain to create a greater impact than if you have vases of mixed blooms dotted about all over the place.

Try the effect of all pink flowers at a Sunday morning gathering. There are endless sizes, shapes and varieties of pink flowers growing in our gardens, or obtainable from a good florist, and a hostess can gain great éclat by planning the flowers, drinks and eats in the one colour, using a pink cloth. Think of the delightful effect of large vases of tall pink Larkspurs, shorter pink Godetia, with pink sweet peas and pink cornflowers. For an important effect, the pink Cleome or Spider Flower is admirable. Easy to grow, but unusual to look at, it always evokes a lot of comment; placed with large grey artichoke or cotton thistle leaves, it can appear magnificent.

For your cocktail party on a hot summer's evening, you might enjoy arranging all white, or white and green, flowers, for these give a wonderfully cooling effect. Bowls of green apples, dishes of green olives, cheese-filled celery on lettuce leaves, all add to the effect, which can be accentuated by green candles. On such an occasion, you could criss-cross the tablecloth with green ribbon, weighing down the ends with bunches of greenery pinned on. As a cocktail, try serving Czar's Emerald, made from equal portions of vodka and crème de menthe. This drink can be made longer by adding carbonated or tonic water and ice. Another green drink could be a gin-and-lime swizzle.

Cutlery, china and glasses can be hired if necessary from local caterers or big stores, as also can trestle tables, if you do not possess tables large enough from which to serve. These trestle tables should be completely covered with cloths or sheets, both of which can be tinted if required. Do try giving a lift to the table by covering several boxes or tins with white or coloured paper; these, placed at different intervals and heights on the table, create a three-dimensional effect to the setting.

Buffet Tables

Many practised hostesses are finding a buffet party more acceptable to their friends than the cocktail party. I must admit I enjoy these much more myself ; there is a casualness about them even if it is studied. As a guest you know you are not going to starve or hover from one leg to another ; as hostess you relax in the knowledge that guests can either help themselves or be helped at the serving table and, providing enough sitting-out places are available, you or your guests can wander from group to group.

The flower decorations for a buffet table are better placed high, either an arrangement in the centre with the drinks at one end and food at the other, or a tall decoration at each end of the serving table with the food placed centrally.

I have seen a well-laden buffet table placed in front of the fireplace with decorations on the mantelshelf, and since a lot of the interest will be centred around this table the flower scheme should be well accentuated.

Another excellent idea is to give a wine-and-cheese party. I first met this ideal method of entertaining a number of friends when I was travelling in the U.S.A. ; but it has become very popular in England since wine has become more readily available.

One of the many advantages of the wine-and-cheese party is that you can stage it for any number of guests and at almost any hour, the favourite times being 6–8 p.m., or from 8 p.m. onwards, or after the theatre. For a small gathering, you need only offer two kinds of wine, a red and a white (or a sweet and a dry), with an assortment of cheeses. If you reckon on three glasses of wine (half a bottle) each, and about a quarter of a pound of cheese, quarter of a pound of biscuits or two slices of French bread each, you can plan your consumption well in advance according to the number of guests you expect to entertain. It is always better to err on the generous side—some appetites may be bigger than others ; and most of the left-over food items can be absorbed into the household, whilst, if you wish it, the wines will as a rule be supplied on a sale-or-return basis by the local wine merchant, who will often lend you the necessary glasses.

Serve your cheeses cut up in small cubes on boards if possible, each board or plate bearing a little flag stating the name of the cheese thereon. The cheeses, which could be Cheddar, Caerphilly, Lancashire and Wensleydale, can be arranged on a side-table together with large plates of cut French bread and pats of butter. You might also include Danish rye bread and digestive and dry biscuits ; it is the fun of choosing different items which can make such a party a success and it is better to supply a wide variety so that guests can go from one

to the other. For a larger party I would include a greater variety of wines, perhaps Hock, Vin Rosé, white Macon, Beaujolais, with port and sherry, and some of the stronger cheeses such as Stilton, Dorset Blue Vinny or Danish Blue, or the piquant-flavoured Blue Cheshire.

You may also like to try some of my own additions to such a party—a choice of cheese dips and spreads. Try mashing with a fork a portion of Lancashire cheese (this has a loose and flaky texture) with white wine, a few drops of onion juice and some salad cream until the mixture becomes creamy. This makes an ideal spread for slices of French bread which can either be served on the bread or left in the dish for guests to help themselves.

Another tasty cheese spread can be made by mixing a cupful of grated Cheddar with two tablespoonsful of butter, half a cup of chopped Indian chutney and half a teaspoonful of made mustard. Mix all together until smooth and serve with crackers, toasted sticks or bread.

Cheese puff balls can be served either as appetisers or at the end of your party. To make these you require : 2 egg whites, $\frac{1}{4}$ lb. grated Parmesan cheese, $\frac{1}{4}$ teaspoonful of salt, $\frac{1}{8}$ teaspoonful dry mustard, fine crumbs.

Beat the egg whites until stiff. Combine the grated Parmesan cheese, salt, mustard and mix into the egg whites. Form into balls the size of large grapes, then roll in fine crumbs. Fry in deep fat and drain on crumpled paper napkins. Serve speared on toothpicks. The above amount makes about eighteen balls.

An alternative to the above and as a parting gesture, try a cheese fondue. If made and served at table, the whole procedure can be entertaining ; in fact men love taking a hand in making such a dish. You will need : a garlic clove, 12 ozs. Swiss cheese, 2 tablespoons flour, a tablespoon salt, freshly ground black pepper, $1\frac{1}{2}$ cups white wine, 2 ozs. Kirsch or Cognac, a loaf of French bread.

Rub a $2\frac{1}{2}$ quart earthenware casserole with a cut clove of garlic. Coarsely grate Swiss cheese and mix it with the flour, salt and pepper. Heat the wine in

27

the casserole over very low heat, preferably at the table. When the wine is hot but not boiling, add the cheese, a little at a time, adding more as it melts. Keep stirring over low heat and when all is softly bubbling, add the Kirsch or Cognac. Cut a loaf of crusty French bread into cubes so that each piece has a bit of crust. Each guest spears pieces of bread with a fork and dunks them in the dish, giving the fondue a stir. The fondue should be kept warm, but not hot. If it becomes too thick, add more wine, heated. This amount serves twelve.

Piles of bread in baskets, bowls of radishes, fingers of celery and cheese straws can be placed around, although I prefer concentrating on the cheese, the wines and, of course, the decorations. The decorations, whether of fruit, flowers or gay tablecloths and candles in wine bottles, will all add atmosphere. If your setting will allow it, try to include vines or trailing creepers into your decorative scheme and combine these with bunches and bunches of grapes together with ears of wheat and barley and bright, but not formal, flowers. Pottery, pewter and wood are ideal as containers or additions for bright flowers, such as Daisies, Sunflowers, Marigolds, Dahlias and Gladioli. If your home setting is more formal, however, there could be nothing more lovely than grapes and vines and a few flowers spilling over from the rims of Dresden or Meissen china compôte dishes. Candlelight, whether from candelabra or Chianti bottles, is ideally suited to the mellowing atmosphere of a wine-and-cheese party.

For those who like curry, and there is an increasing number who are acquiring the taste for spicy dishes, nothing is more inviting than a curry party.

I suggest that three different curries be offered ; these, together with bowls of rice and plates of popadums, dishes of chutney, etc., can be laid out on a long table from which guests can help themselves. Strings of onions, fruits and vegetable arrangements are all suitable at such a party, but the décor can only be decided after considering the background. Obviously strings of onions would appear incongruous on a table in a formal room, but would be in keeping should the curry be served in the kitchen. So many kitchens are attractive and have character today, that it is becoming quite popular to eat in the kitchen after drinks have been offered in the more formal rooms. Onions, seed heads, leaves, fruits and gourds all make attractive curry-party decorations, and I would suggest that chilled white wine, cider, beer or soft drinks be offered, since spirits are not as a rule drunk with curry.

Do make plenty of the basic curry sauce ; bowls of this, placed around the room, will prove very welcome, for potato crisps, pieces of cauliflower or fingers of toast can all be dipped in it and enjoyed.

We all know there are many variations of curry, but no one could fail to enjoy the following recipes which were given to me by my good friend Mofiz Ulla, who now spreads goodwill with his curry at the New Assam Restaurant in London's Chelsea. To make the basic sauce you need : 1 tablespoon curry powder, 1 teaspoon paprika, 6 bay leaves, 1 cinnamon stick, 8 cloves, 3 cardomen seeds (crushed), 2 large onions, 4 ozs. margarine, salt and Chilli powder to taste, 2 pints stock or water.

Chop onions and fry until golden in fat, add all powder ingredients and stir over gentle heat until cooked. Add stock little by little, simmering all the while ; allow to simmer for ten minutes, then add all other ingredients and simmer for twenty minutes, making sure it does not boil. You are now ready to add the main ingredient, which can be eggs, prawns, or beef.

For prawn curry, take one third of your curry sauce and put into another pan, add three tomatoes cut in quarters and cook ten minutes, then add half a pound of shelled prawns and cook for further fifteen minutes.

For an egg curry, use the same sauce, dropping in six hard-boiled eggs, cut in half lengthwise.

For beef curry, cook in this manner : $1\frac{1}{2}$ tablespoons curry powder, $\frac{1}{2}$ teaspoon Chilli powder, $\frac{1}{2}$ tablespoon paprika, 4 cardomen seeds (crushed), 8 bay leaves, 10 cloves, $\frac{1}{4}$ teaspoon powdered caraway seeds, 1 cinnamon stick, 4 ozs. margarine, 1 lb. onions, 3 lbs. beef cut in small cubes.

Clean and chop onions and fry in fat. Add all powder and spices and mix well, drop beef into mixture and stir over low heat until all is covered with spices. Cover and allow to remain on gentle heat for twenty minutes, shaking occasionally. Add stock to cover ingredients by one inch. Stir well and allow to cook slowly until beef is tender.

Use the same basic sauce to serve with this beef.

To cook rice, use : $\frac{1}{2}$ lb. Patna rice, 1 pint water, pepper and salt. Simmer until water is absorbed, then place the rice in a colander and run warm water through it, afterwards placing it in a shallow dish in the oven to dry.

I guarantee, if you like curry and follow the above recipes, adding some atmosphere with unusual decorations, your curry parties will become the talk of the town !

Many other special type buffet parties come to my mind. Imagine, for instance, a party where only fish dishes are offered. The theme here could be emphasised with plant or flower arrangement made in shells ; fish net, scallop and other shells could all be introduced on the serving table, some of the more shallow type being used to hold tit-bits.

As I pointed out earlier, the purpose of this book is not to tell you how to give your party, but to stimulate your own ideas to flow. You may like to hear of a hurried change I was once forced to make two days before the date of a party I was giving in a new studio I had taken. The walls had been freshly plastered and decorated, but two days before the party the hardly dry plaster fell down. There was no time to do anything but wash over the rough remains of the wall, so I revised entirely the scheme I had planned and decided on a Chinese setting and food. To lower the ceiling height I hung a number of Chinese lanterns on several strings criss-crossed from side to side of the room, and burned scented joss-sticks to combat the smell of the plaster. Tall, swerving branches which gave lovely silhouettes in the shadows were fixed into jars, and we all enjoyed eating small dishes of sweet and sour pork, noodles, fruit salads and glacéed fruits, served with warm rice wine. I had not warned the guests of my sudden change of plans and so for those who might not like pork there was a variety of patties as well as a chicken-and-potato salad, and the usual drinks. However, most guests wanted to try the Chinese method of cooking small pieces of pork, and they found it delicious.

Coffee and soft drinks should also be available at buffet parties and sweets such as sorbets, rhum baba, ice creams or trifles, in addition to *petits fours*, peppermint creams and candied fruits—always acceptable to those who have a sweet tooth.

Special Occasions

Special Occasions

WHAT a wonderful chance there is to show skill and expression with flower decorations when faced with the opportunity to 'do the flowers' for any special occasion. It may be a birthday, a wedding, a christening, a homecoming, Easter or Hallowe'en, or any of the dozens of very special occasions we are called upon to celebrate from time to time. Whatever the event, I do suggest you let the flowers help tell the story; play up the theme, even if you suppress some of your personal likes. This means that even if you are fond of pink Chrysanthemums and beautiful lace cloths, it would prove more interesting if your floral arrangement for, shall we say, a Guy Fawkes party featured bolt upright Bulrushes to represent rockets, some of them glittered to resemble sparklers, placed as the background to a grouping of fiery red Nerines and gold and yellow Chrysanthemums, balanced low down with pieces of barkwood twigs and other items.

Guy Fawkes parties can be held in the evening for grown-ups, although they have now become chiefly associated with the younger members of the family, and are often celebrated, as darkness falls, in the garden where the bonfire reigns supreme. A good idea here is to offer mugs of cocoa, buns and hot sausages to be eaten by the glare of the fireworks, and a lot of fun can be had from cooking potatoes in the ashes of the fire. (We always parboil ours first.) Parents and nannies will call for children as the fire dies down and it is then that a hot punch can be offered to the grown-ups in the house, where the appropriate flowers will be appreciated. So when giving a special-occasion party, try to emphasise the motif with your flower arrangements; in this way the memory of the event will linger on.

The Festival of Harvest is another occasion for which many parties are given and most hostesses love this theme, for it allows plenty of opportunity to display the fruits of the garden and fields in abundance. Gay coloured flowers, fruits, berries, vegetables, grasses, wheat and barley can all be featured and this plant material usually appears more effective when placed in brass, pewter, stone, pottery, wooden or basketware containers.

Flower arrangements for Easter festivities are usually interpreted with white flowers, so Arum and Easter Lilies are often used, being symbols of purity and dignity. Tall, upward-surging yet simple arrangements, signifying ascendancy, are favoured at this time of the year.

Birthday party flowers should of course compliment the person whose party

● *An arrangement featuring wood for a Guy Fawkes party. This*
'bonfire' of tree wood piled on a skip basket lid has
Bulrush 'rockets' and glittered onion seed head 'sparklers'.
Dried bracken and other leaves are added lower down,
and catherine wheels and crackers complete the design.

• *An aspirational Easter design for a modern setting is made by placing six Arum Lilies on a pin-holder surrounded by stones in a tilted pottery bowl.*

• *A tall, narrow-necked container holds a simple arrangement of Easter Lilies. A bowl of grapes completes the setting.*

34

● *For a christening celebration cover the table*
with pink or blue ninon and choose
simple flowers such as the Pinks, Sweetheart
Roses and Gypsophila in this cherubic
container.   Do not forget dishes
of traditional sugar almonds.

● *Here's a suggestion for an arrangement in church, where light-coloured*
flowers in an easily distinguished pattern should be the aim.
This triangular style is made by placing the straight stems
of Iris down the centre, allowing the Tulips
to flow out at the sides and front.   Leaves are
tucked in close to the wire-netting holding the flowers in place.

37

● *For a special tea party—a one-colour*
  scheme of pink Schízostylis
  and grasses grouped in a pink-
  and-white pottery shell with pink
  Asters and crimson Pinks.
  The china and cloth repeat the pink theme.

● *A chimney-piece is an ideal spot for flowers at any reception.*
  Here Arctic Ice Delphiniums are arranged with coral
  pink Roses and lime-green Dock and Iris seed pods.
  Large Funkia leaves are inserted into the centre, and the
  container was a painted cake tin filled with wet
  Florapak and wire which held the stems firmly in place.

● *Pale pink satin covers the table for this wedding celebration setting.   Deeper pink Roses
emphasised with bows of pale green ribbon are held in a white
china container ; white china cherubs frivol along the length of the table.
The Posies of white Heather are surrounded by green ribbon frills.*

● *The outline of this unsophisticated pedestal design for an early September wedding reception is made with fine Silver Spray Michaelmas Daisies. Lower down, the pink Apple Blossom variety surround the pink Belladonna Lilies placed in the centre.*

41

it is, so flowers must be chosen to suit them and not yourself. For a demure young girl's 'coming out' party, you could try to emphasise the background by arranging large bunches of Queen Anne's Lace, Marguerites, Pinks, Cornflowers, Candytuft or Sweet Peas, or any unsophisticated flowers in pastel tints. Tie them up with large bows of pink or apple-green ribbon ; accentuate them by their quantity, for these simple flowers have no exotic qualities. On the other hand, a similar event staged for an eighteen-year-old outdoor girl, probably a keen young horsewoman, would call for arrangements made with branches, grasses and field flowers. If the event is more formal, try designs using more precious flowers in elegant containers.

Twenty-first birthday party decorations are planned round the theme of the coming of age. Naturally the figure 21 is emphasised on cake, candles and decorations. Cards and congratulatory telegrams can be prominently displayed and the buffet or party table flanked by large cut-out cardboard keys, a symbol (even though not always significant today) of the recipient being allowed the freedom of the house. The flowers on such occasions can be arranged to suit the person, or, if a girl, the colour of her dress. On one such occasion I made a tree composed of bare twigs from the garden, on which I hung twenty-one keys, all previously gilded. After the toast had been drunk and the cake cut, the young person concerned was asked to choose one of the keys which would open a box containing something she dearly wanted. To help her choose we all voiced 'You are warm' or 'You are cold', accompanied of course by sips of champagne. As she approached making her decision we all cried 'no' or 'take the lower or higher one' until finally she made her determined choice and, of course, as previously arranged, it was the right key which opened the box containing a present.

When planning designs for a gathering after a Christening party, rather simple flowers are called for. Choose pink or blue or pastel-tinted flowers and place them in unsophisticated vases. Many florists supply pottery or basketware cradles, which look delightful filled with Forget-me-nots, Polyantha Roses, pink Chrysanthemums and Baby's Breath (Gypsophila). For your party, plan a christening cake over which hovers an artificial stork, and if you possess some of those porcelain figurines of storks or herons, you could hang from the beaks little bundles filled with sugar almonds. Place large bowls filled with sugar almonds around the room ; in fact, as a gesture why not do as is done on the Continent, give each guest a small bag or package containing sugar almonds, a symbol of the coins and gratuities distributed by the godfather at christenings in earlier times.

A christening is not a long ceremony in church, though it is important to those who take part in it. Some people like the memory of a flower-bedecked font, but do make certain first that there is no objection to this. A delightful decoration can be made by fixing round the font a roll of chicken wire filled with moss, into which small flowers in season are inserted. Another idea is to string or wire together a number of meat-paste pots, fixing them in a circle round the font. Fill each little pot with water, adding flowers and trailing leaves.

Flowers for a wedding are quite special and come into a category all their own. Here I would like to stress the importance of contacting your florist early for such items as head-dress, bouquet and bridesmaids' bouquets. The making of bouquets is a professional job and only a professional can do it well, so, no matter how keen you are to try it for yourself, my advice is—*don't*. It is always better not to tread into the domain of the florist ; she has gained her skill by years of hard work and practice, and she will be much more your friend should you need her help at some future time, if you leave her to do the job for which she has been trained.

Most florists will arrange the flowers for the reception and the church, if requested to do so, but if you feel you can manage this yourself and would like to do it, then there are a few principles to be borne in mind. Always consult the Vicar before planning your church decorations ; the church is his responsibility and he may not approve of some decorative schemes. Some incumbents do not allow flowers on the altar, some do ; but in all cases if they are approached seriously and the wishes of the bride explained, they are usually most co-operative.

Flowers for the altar should not be too imposing and should be white ; but yellow, pale pink, mauve or coral can be used for large pedestal arrangements for each side of the chancel steps, or you might try choosing flowers which will combine with the overall colour scheme of the bridal retinue. The bride may be wearing white and the bridesmaids yellow ; then employ these two colours in your flower arrangements. On the other hand it may be an all-white wedding, with the bridegroom in uniform, in which case you might introduce his regimental colours into the flower scheme. Alternatively, keep to an all-white scheme ; but always try to avoid buying the flowers without previous consultation with the bride.

A similar colour scheme to that of the flowers in the church can be introduced in the reception rooms, and an elegant arrangement of white flowers, placed on the mantelshelf or on a pedestal, will form a lovely framework for the bride and groom as they stand waiting to receive the congratulations of family and friends. As a change, I once used a white birdcage on a tall stand for a young friend's wedding, allowing sprays of pink and white Carnations to flow out of it. A pink ribbon bow was fixed to the top, encircling a delicate white dove which held a ring in its beak and peered downwards. Inside the cage, surrounded by the Carnations, was the bird's mate. All the guests loved the idea, and it is yours to copy.

Wedding anniversaries call for celebration parties and it is a good idea to introduce, with floral decorations, some of the symbols that are attached to these anniversaries. In arranging flowers for a twenty-fifth wedding anniversary celebration, try to introduce silver, perhaps by using white flowers in a silver bowl or vase tied with a silver tinsel ribbon. A golden-wedding celebration might feature golden-coloured flowers. There are so many in this colour range from Chrysanthemums, Roses, Gerberras, Carnations, Dahlias, Gladioli and Day Lilies. These could be placed in either a new golden-wedding-present vase, or in a vase or bowl which was an original wedding present, for sentiment's sake. Alternatively any existing vase or basket can easily be covered with gold paint. This is definitely an occasion that should be emphasised with as much gold as possible, so buy some gold lamé or gauze and use as a tablecloth. Buy candles on which the number 50 is marked in gold. (Any good store will get these for you.) Celebrate with a cake bound in a gold frill and use gold-paper doilies. Allow the number 50 to remain prominent, even if you cut this out in cardboard and cover it with gold paint. And of course champagne or sparkling wine is a must.

So much for gold, but think of all the ideas that can be exploited when planning flowers for other wedding anniversaries. The symbols are as follows : for the tenth, tin ; the twelfth, silk ; the fifteenth, crystal ; the twentieth, china ; the thirtieth, pearl ; the fortieth, ruby—what a chance here for flower displays ; while, if any two people reach this blessed state, the sixtieth wedding anniversary has diamonds for its symbol. If after all this you still want to be original, we can go back to the first, second and third anniversaries which call for cotton, paper and leather respectively !

Formal and Informal

Formal and Informal

IT is not easy to generalise when giving suggestions for formal and informal table settings, for there are so many variations. However, it is agreed that when flowers are used on the table, they should be considered as part of the whole setting, and not as an individual flower arrangement. The size of the table, as well as the colour and texture of china, should be taken into consideration, and the table coverings, whether cloths or mats, should all play their part either in accentuating or complementing the colours or theme of the flowers.

Flowers for the more formal dinner party, whether small or large, should preferably be of the more precious or fine nature to combine with the best china or glass. Roses, Carnations, Orchids, Freesias, Camellias, are suitable choices, although those who are gardeners will have a wide choice of personally grown preferences. The flowers can be grouped high round the tops of candelabra, or arranged low in the centre of the table. Variations can take the form of having two small groups at each end of the table, or individual arrangements at each place setting, but however the flowers are arranged, colouring is very important.

If the colouring of the china is not strong (it may be white with a gold band), the colouring of the flowers can be allowed to dominate ; for instance, in autumn, scarlet Carnations bursting from a foundation of green Hydrangeas, or in spring, orange Clivias grouped with green grapes. Freesias with Grevillia foliage are also lovely in spring. Camellias add elegance to any table and more particularly if you possess the fine china service which features this exquisite bloom.

Water Lilies and Begonias are favourites for floating arrangements in summer, although the petals of Water Lilies should be held back while warm candle-wax is poured round the stamens, otherwise they will close up at night. Ivy interwoven with chunks of glass will give a cool effect, while colourful fruit arranged in a sophisticated pyramid fashion will prove very effective at a formal dinner party.

Containers should be elegant and of fine china, glass or silver for the more formal occasion, although a dish similar in pattern to that of the dinner service is often a good choice. Very little of the container is seen, so a shallow glass bowl or a silver cake basket combine with most appointments.

The ideas for arranging flowers on tables are endless, but do remember that they should either be placed high enough so that guests can look under them (as

● *Small conch shells hold dry grasses, pink Acrocliniums and Statice on a table laid for an informal luncheon party at which fish is the main course. The sea horses on the linen mats perpetuate the theme.*

● *A few exotic flowers enliven a table laid*
for casual entertaining.
Here, three blooms of Strelitzia Reginae
(Birds of Paradise) are held on a pin-holder
in a dish of water on a large platter,
with fruit arranged to hide the container.
These long-lasting flowers,
though expensive, are a good investment.

● *Tree-like decorations are novel and easy to make. Nail a deep tin lid to one end of a dowel stick, then fix the other end with Plasticine into a flower pot which is then filled with stones, plaster and moss. The flowers are inserted into a dome of wire-netting in a container which rests on the tin.*

● *The silhouette of a tall branch has a great decorative appeal.*
This design for an informal family gathering
was completed by a few Dahlias held on a large pin-holder.

● *Green Funkia leaves emphasise this modern design*
with Gladioli in a black dish.

● *The cool atmosphere created by this arrangement of glass*
in shades of green on a pale
green cloth makes it a perfect
design for a hot day.
The summer Jasmine is inserted into damp moss.

● *Sturdy, long-lasting Anthuriums decorate this table*
laid for an informal meal on the terrace.
The container in which they are held on a
pin-holder is hidden by a piece
of root wood, the base covered with moss.

● *A casual arrangement of flowers for tea time.* *These pink and crimson Asters are easily grown from seed.*

● *A basket of pale lemon-yellow Iris, surrounded low down*
with Kale leaves and green apples, makes
the centre-piece for another informal luncheon table.

55

● *An all-green table arrangement of grasses,*
  Fennel, Fern, Mint and Rosemary,
  held firm by wire-netting, made to
  match green-patterned Royal Worcester china.

● *Red Carnations rising from a bed of pale green Hydrangea*
heads, held by wire-netting in a shallow glass bowl,
make an effective colour scheme for this
formal dinner table, completed with red candles.

● *Pale coral tuberose Begonias in an unusual container*
which has been made from a pair of clam
shells fixed together with cement.

● *For an intimate occasion—pink Roses*
and red cherries held in a small dish with wire-netting,
and placed on a silver salver.

● *An arrangement for a friendly tea party—*
two sprays of wild green Spurge
on a pin-holder behind a
purple Venetian glass bird standing
in a glass bowl filled with green grapes.

● *This formal arrangement of Arum Lilies*
is suitable for the head of a stairway
or the corner of a large room.
Notice how the flowers flow
forward over the rim of the container.

at a banquet), or low enough to be seen over. Candles can give unobtrusive height to a table arrangement—think of colour, size (the flower arrangement can be one-sixth the size of the table) and suitability in relation to the whole setting.

For the less formal occasions, annual garden flowers, such as Cornflowers, African Daisies, Larkspur, Pinks and many others, are very suitable and could be in keeping with your less precious china and cutlery. Perennial flowers, such as Marguerites, Golden Rod and Michaelmas Daisies, can all be successfully featured as decorations for the informal table, especially when they are coupled with containers from the range of those in pewter, pottery, coarse china, chunky glass or wood.

Bright scarlet Geraniums in modern pottery containers would be gay and ideal for an alfresco lunch on the terrace, as would a basket of green cabbage leaves with apples and a few yellow flowers. Daffodils fixed on a pin-holder in a dish of water standing in a tray full of moss, stones and tree wood would provide a lovely picture for an informal spring table-setting, especially if you used a pale apple-green cloth together with wooden-handled cutlery. Flower pots can be washed over with a thick solution of Alabastine (from the household stores) and be turned into casual plant or flower containers, while all kinds of unusual utensils filled with flowers can be made the centre of attraction for a casual luncheon or dinner table.

For Teenagers

For Teenagers

ACTION, I suggest, is the operative word for teenage parties ; it is the age when one is vitally interested in anything and everything that is happening, and keen to be doing something towards the fun. Action can start with the young people making their own party decorations, for many are more clever than their elders at devising interesting flower arrangements and clever backgrounds, their ideas usually veering towards the original. An invitation to a Valentine party, a Hallowe'en party, a Square Dance, a Travel Film party or a Competition Ramble will not only evoke great interest in the guests, but will also give wonderful opportunities to the young hostess or her parents to devise unusual decorations.

For a Valentine party a delightfully apposite idea would be to use hearts cut out from red art paper as a decorative motif throughout, centred with a white paper doily on which a bunch of Violets is placed. Flower posies nestling in huge swirls or bows of tulle or ribbon and displayed at strategic points in the room also look very effective. Sandwiches can be heart-shaped, too—easily managed with a sharp tin biscuit-cutter. Other suggestions : a tray of small, heart-shaped cakes covered in pink, white, mauve and yellow icing arranged on lacy doilies and interspersed with tiny flower posies ; a large iced cake, either heart-shaped or oblong, to simulate an old Valentine card, decorated with a lacy paper border and some sentimental words piped on in icing of a contrasting colour ; dishes of crystallised violets and rose leaves. These can be purchased at most confectioners, but you may like to make them yourself.

The method is to place in a small screw-top bottle three teaspoonfuls of gum-arabic (crystals, not powder) covered with three tablespoonfuls of rose or orange water. Leave two or three days to dissolve into a sticky glue, shaking the bottle occasionally. Dip the violets or rose petals into this solution, drain, then dredge lightly two or three times with castor sugar until each flower is well covered, and dry off in a warm place on greaseproof paper. Twenty-four hours in the linen cupboard is usually enough. Store in the dark, preferably in a cardboard box. A little vegetable colouring in the gum-arabic solution will

● *This decorative theme for a pirate or seaside party uses a treasure chest overflowing with necklaces, bracelets, rings and coins against a beachcomber background of a fishing-net, sea fern, shells and coral.*

● Hallowe'en Party decorations can be great fun.   Here cat masks, broomsticks
and lanterns are used in a colour scheme of yellow, orange and black.
The scarecrow, made from a melon, an apple, cucumbers and beans,
is the centre-piece of a design of yellow chrysanthemums, wheat and bracken.

● *Another name for Hallowe'en is Apple Night—from the old custom of ducking for apples. A variety of this game is to bite at apples suspended from ribbons (see p. 135), with your hands behind your backs. Cider, nuts and walnut cake go well with this idea, and roasting chestnuts will add to the fun.*

67

● *A visit to the ballet followed by tea or supper is a good excuse for a party.*
  Here a frilly lace petticoat representing a tutu round pink
  Carnations in a brandy glass recaptures the spirit of the dance.
  Ballet shoes, pink candles and fondants complete
  the theme, which is sure to be appreciated by guests who like dancing.

● This 'tree' of Marigolds is made on a cone-shaped framework of wire-netting
filled with wet newspaper. The cone stands on a tray edged with leaves,
and the flowers are inserted through the wire. The table-cloth
is straw-coloured hessian, and the brown bottles of
Coca-Cola in a plaited-straw basket complete the colour scheme.

69

● Sometimes you have so many guests that you have to hire a large room or
hall for your party.   This design could brighten
a dark wall or gloomy corner in the largest place.   Stems of yellow
Solidago (Golden Rod) are inserted into a large potato (see p. 132), and green
leaves with short stems of Achillia and berries are added in the centre.

● *An inexpensive decoration for younger guests*
can be made from a rope of apples and
leaves hung on the wall.
Wire the apples as shown on p. 135 and
twist with the leaves round a piece of rope.

● *An arrangement like this—pink Sedum spectabile (on a pin-holder) and large grey stones, cunningly lit by an unusual grey pottery lamp—will be dramatically effective in a dark corner.*

● *This amusing informal decoration is made by sticking*
Daisies, Chrysanthemums or any hard-stemmed
flowers into a marrow.
The marrow is surrounded by red and
green peppers and held firm by a large pin-holder.

73

● *Many teenagers enjoy making modern flower arrangements.*
Here, for a late summer party at which soft drinks
are served, is a design of orange Montbretias
and Lilies held on a pin-holder in a shallow green
pottery dish. Coloured gourds and
pottery figures are attractive additions to the design.

give the flowers a more cheerful appearance, but care should be taken not to use too much, or the result will be most unnatural.

The greatest fun of all would be to invite the young people in pairs to make their own pancakes. Clear the kitchen of all unnecessary impedimenta and provide a large bowl of batter, a small ladle, two thick frying pans, a dish of cooking fat, a pile of plates and a large jar of St. Valentine's jam (that is, ordinary jam with a heart-shaped label !) for putting on the pancakes when cooked. The excitement of the guests as they queue up for their turn will be enormous. I have tried out this idea myself; some guests tossed their pancakes (some successfully, some not) and a few burnt theirs. Most of the boys showed great pride in their cooking abilities, swopping kitchen stories to prove it.

Few parties intrigue the young more than a Hallowe'en party, on the eve of All Saints' Day (31st October), when witches are supposed to career round the skies on their broomsticks, guided by mysterious lights, such as Jack o' Lanterns. Although a number of the superstitions attached to this day are now forgotten, a few of the customs show no sign of dying out. One of these is the cutting out of spooky faces on the skins of marrows, melons or swedes, and placing a light inside (to frighten the witch). Another favourite Hallowe'en party game is bobbing for apples, although, to avoid the spoiling of party dresses, the apples are now usually hung from a line of string, the players, with their hands behind their backs, having to bite the apples until eaten.

Lights, spooky faces, mysterious messages, corn, wheat, yellow flowers and fruit and vegetable arrangements all accentuate the party atmosphere and a few mysterious games (such as ' Murder ') could be included. A cup of steaming soup, served from a black cauldron, might be given to the departing guests.

For a Square Dance, providing there is room, the young host or hostess could arrange huge bunches of grasses and Marguerites as the decorative motif. Waste-paper baskets covered with sheet music could hold bottles of milk or soft drinks ready to be served. Or, as milk is proving a very fashionable drink with young people, a milk bar might be arranged with various flavourings added to the milk ; this could be a centre of attraction. Swags of greenery tied up with ribbon or bare branches from which hang oranges and lemons fixed with wire, apples stuck with flowers, will all give atmosphere to such a party. When dancing and strenuous games are offered the ' eats ' should be fairly substantial and savoury. Items such as dips (see p. 150) and sausages and two-decker sandwiches are always popular.

It is fun to arrange a Film Travel party during the winter, showing slides or films of holidays. If these have been spent abroad, accentuate the theme by introducing into your décor some atmosphere evocative of the country visited. For instance, if this happened to be Spain, use red, purple and yellow flowers in containers swathed with red satin capes and pin a few Travel to Spain posters to the walls. Figurines of bulls and matadors, if you have them, pairs of castanets, a doll dressed as a Spanish dancer—all will help to conjure up this hot and exciting country. Small dishes of Spanish Paella could be served on such an occasion. If, on the other hand, an English seaside holiday is to be the subject of the party, green plants, fish-net and travel posters will give the right atmosphere, while the theme can be carried further by serving an interesting fish dish in scallop shells from a table strewn with smaller sea shells.

Young people only need one idea to light the spark which fires many more in their own minds. A theme of ski-ing decorations, mountaineering, or an Italian background décor with Italian food offerings—all present a touch of originality, while in each case guests can be asked to dress appropriately in ski suits, Italian dress, and so on.

One young girl I know took her friends on a flower ramble. A competition was arranged, the winner being the one who named the greatest number of wild flowers during the prescribed ramble, and after a picnic tea, all were asked to pick enough flowers, twigs and leaves to make an arrangement. On the return to the house these were placed in a bath of water to revive, while tins, cups, saucers or other containers were prepared with crumpled wire on a trestle table in the garden. The arrangements were then made and were finally judged by the parents. You never saw such activity and interest, and some very good flower arrangements resulted.

In the winter dancing is always popular with teenagers, though this of course will depend upon whether a spare room can be given over to such activity. A record player is a necessity, and a few Paul Joneses, interspersed with the latest mode of dancing, whether it be Scottish reels, rock and roll, cha-cha or country dancing or the waltz and quick step, will very quickly help the guests to mix.

Of course, an accomplished guitarist or popular singer will always prove popular at teenagers' parties, so if you are able to you should hire one, if only for fifteen minutes or half an hour ; it will make your party so much more appealing. Do allow the decorations to shine : a basket of rosy apples framed with cabbage leaves can be most effective, or a large ornament can be ' played up ' with flowers. Paper hats or masks will also make a party go with a swing. All kinds of masks, whether they be owl-shaped or catlike, representing butterflies or skeletons, can be obtained quite cheaply from Ellisdons, 37–39 High

Holborn, London ; they also supply an immense variety of party novelties, balloons and musical noise-makers.

One exciting idea, thought of for a fruit-picking party, was to gild the leaves of a pineapple head. On each protruding knob of the fruit I placed a bright-coloured bead pierced through with a pin. Inserted in the top of a brandy glass, the pineapple looked like a huge jewel out of the Arabian Nights. The guests had previously been invited to pick fruit in the orchard and all were asked to wear jeans and shirts.

Games are popular with some young people, although it is the game of the moment which is the last word at such parties, and most teenagers know more about these than parents. Cider, wine and milk punches are popular as drinks with the young, so on arrival welcome them with a cold punch (see p. 147) in summer, or a hot one (see p. 146) in winter.

SOME INDOOR GAMES FOR TEENAGERS

Advertisements

This is a game that needs some preparation beforehand. Cut out well-known advertisement illustrations from magazines and newspapers, then snip away any obvious trade marks which might serve as clues. Paste the cuttings on large sheets of paper, number them, and pin up around the room in suitable positions so that your guests can see the pictures easily. (Keep a list of the correct answers yourself.) Each player is given a piece of paper and pencil, and has to make a list of the name of the product and also the maker's name against the corresponding numbers. Award marks accordingly.

Murder

Any number of players can take part in this game, but unless you have a very large house it is best to limit them to eight or ten, otherwise it will be rather difficult to baffle the detective. Each player draws a folded slip of paper from a hat or bag ; one of these is marked with a cross, another with a circle, the rest being blank. The person who draws the cross is the murderer and keeps silent, while the one who gets the circle becomes the detective, who makes himself known to the company. All the lights are turned out and the players (except for the detective) disperse. The murderer in due course chooses his victim and whispers to him (or her) ' You are dead '. The victim screams loudly, which is a signal for the lights to be turned on. The players must ' stay put ', wherever they are, with the exception of the murderer, who must try and get as far as possible from the body before the lights go up, or he will be seen moving away by the detective, who now hurries to the scene of the crime. After he has noted the positions of everybody, he proceeds to question them. The murderer is the only one who is allowed to lie ; the others must answer absolutely truthfully any questions put to them by the guardian of the law, who has only two chances of asking the direct question, ' Are you the Murderer ? ', unless there are a large number of suspects, in which case he may be permitted to repeat the question once more. If the detective is wrong, it is taken that the murderer has got away with his crime.

Story Spinning

1. The first player starts a story, giving the first sentence only. The second player continues with the next sentence, and so on. Anybody who hesitates or produces an entirely irrelevant addition is counted out.

2. The host starts this story by telling of some article his relation, the Admiral, kept in his cabin, beginning with the letter A. The next player repeats this and adds another item beginning with the letter B, and so on through the alphabet. Anyone who misses a turn is out. One's ancestors need not be admirals ; they can be cooks, butlers, engine drivers, soldiers, etc. Example : ' My ancestor the Admiral had an Aldis lamp in his cabin,' says the first player. ' My ancestor the Admiral had an Aldis lamp and a very strong Bosun as well,' says the second player. The next repeats all this and adds (maybe) ' And the Capstan he kept was not all that it might be.'

Fun for Children

Fun for Children

COLOUR and presentation are two important ingredients when planning a party for the very young, so aim for colourful but simple eats and drinks, and present all these items in an unusual manner. On arrival, introduce something moving, such as toy birds twirling round a series of sticks, a mechanical toy, a goldfish tank, or gas-filled balloons floating up to the ceiling. This will produce immediate wonderment and interest and if you can lead the young guests (perhaps in a 'follow-my-leader' chain) straight to a bran tub, inviting them to take a dip, their 'find'—whether it be a hat, a whistle, or a gun—will evoke an exchange of interest and help them to chatter to each other.

Games are an essential ingredient, although these should not be too complicated. A good idea is to have heaps of sweets available to be handed round between events. In the party rooms remove any prized ornaments or possessions out of reach and make sure all fires are screened. Most important of all, see that the whereabouts of the bathroom is known to adults.

Much of the time can be taken up with the excitement of eating. Cakes and biscuits cut out in animal shapes, or marked with the names of the children, always delight. A large shallow dish filled with a 'lake' of green jelly on which float wafers and sweets to represent sailing boats, is another popular idea. Most attractive of all, perhaps, is a complete centrepiece on the table or sideboard depicting a scene typical of the season of the party. This could be a reindeer chariot travelling over snow made with plaster of Paris or Alabastine, or you could build up a wintry scene on a looking glass, to represent a skating pond, the edges holding twigs of yew or other greenery stuck in Plasticine. Small figures could appear to skate over the ice.

A gaily painted wooden wheelbarrow filled with fruit and bags of sweets is another attractive centrepiece, while any scene such as a farmyard, Noah's Ark, a maypole, Easter chicks, harvesting wagon, or Punch and Judy show on a table—all attract the eyes of the young as quickly as a magnet draws a pin.

Eats for the older children of seven to eleven years can be a little more savoury, and drinks served with a straw add interest. For this age group you might like to fix up a counter covered with sunshades or golf umbrellas. The children could then at a given time take their plates and be served from this counter, retreating to a chair or cushion on the floor to eat.

Another good idea for children of any age is to give them each a cake box as tea time arrives, each box containing an assortment of eats. The children

● *A roundabout centre-piece for the party tea table made on a cakeboard
covered with red paper.   A candlestick holds a wire lamp shade,
bound with red gummed wrapping tape, on which is placed a
pleated frill of red-and-white striped paper.
The plastic horses are fixed on at intersections of the wire.*

● *Plaster powder mixed with water to the consistency*
of treacle and poured into a tray makes a
snowy base on which can be built up a variety
of Christmas scenes for the party table.
This design uses a whitened branch and greenery
for trees, with toy reindeer pulling
Father Christmas and his sleigh full of presents.

● *A toy such as a tin drum makes an ideal centre-piece for a children's Christmas party table. A shallow dish of Marguerites held on a pin-holder stands on top of the drum, and plenty of crackers and small toys make the table gay and inviting.*

● *Tapioca forms the snowy base for this
design in which a spray of pine and
bark wood are held firm in
Plasticine and supported by stones in a flat pottery dish.*

84

● *Here is a design for an Easter decoration—Daffodils*
and Pussy Willow held on a pin-holder in a dish
of water set on a tray.   A piece of bark
hides the dish, and the woolly lamb is fun.

85

● *All sorts of interesting food to amuse and satisfy the young.*

● *A few more ideas for Easter—coloured and
chocolate eggs piled into a plastic
salad shaker, with primroses inserted
through the base into a dish of water.
The egg motif is repeated by china
chicks and sweets in a nest of shavings.*

can sit down at the table already decorated with a centrepiece, each one eating from his or her respective tuck box, containing perhaps sandwiches, biscuits, small cakes, sweets, and an ice-cream tub.

Cakes for children's parties should be of the simple, sponge type ; iced and imaginatively decorated, they can assume an exciting appearance. In case you may like to make some of these yourself, here is a good basic Victoria sponge recipe which will make one 8 in. sandwich or several small cakes ; increase the ingredient amounts as necessary. You will need 4 oz. butter, 4 oz. castor sugar, 4 oz. flour, jam, 2 eggs, $\frac{1}{4}$ teaspoonful baking powder, little milk, castor sugar to dredge. Cream fat and sugar together until light and fluffy. Beat in eggs, adding a little at a time. Sieve flour and baking powder together and fold in lightly, together with a little milk if necessary to give a soft dropping consistency. Put into two greased sandwich tins and bake in moderate oven for 25–30 minutes. When cool, sandwich together with the jam and finally dust with castor sugar. Alternatively, bake in square tins and after icing cut into separate small cakes ; or cut first and cover each piece with icing. Add decorations.

For frosted icing the ingredient proportions are one egg white to 8 oz. icing sugar and 4 tablespoonfuls of water. Put sugar and water into a strong sauce-pan and stir over low heat until sugar is dissolved. Boil to a temperature of 240° F. Beat into this sugar syrup the egg white beaten until stiff ; continue to whisk until the mixture is thick. Add colouring and flavouring as desired. To make glacé icing, put 8 oz. sieved icing sugar into a bowl and add gradually about two tablespoonfuls of warm water until the desired consistency is obtained. Add colouring and flavouring. For coffee flavouring, use coffee essence instead of water.

Drinks, whether Coca-Cola, orange squash, tea or chocolate, can be served separately. Decorations should be gay, but not formal, so try the effect of bunches of balloons, windmills, switches of greenery and ribbon tied to toy trumpets and drums ; while glass bottles filled with smarties or poppets are not only decorative but can be shared out at some time during the party. You may also like to try an idea that used to thrill me as a child, when ' hundreds and thousands ' were shaken out of a sugar sifter on to our bread and butter.

Small paper flags bearing the child's name and stuck into an apple or orange can be a table place favour, and of course the highlight of most children's parties is the prize- or gift-giving. These could be distributed from a ' tree ' of bare branches or greenery and need not be expensive. A small book, a plastic toy, some sweets or a puzzle would all be acceptable and I have successfully tried the trick of labelling each small package ' To be opened at home.' This avoids comparisons being made, and each child wanting another's present.

Something
New

Something New

IN addition to the decorations for a party, which can be planned well in advance, there are a number of other occasions when you may wish to introduce an original note. It may be you are planning a family gathering, or a casual meal for a small group of friends ; perhaps a tea party is part of your day's activities as a finale to a committee meeting. Whatever the occasion, an item which is different, whether it is a coloured cloth, an odd vase or an original design, can prove stimulating to friends and family alike.

Try putting red cherries in a clear glass bottle or storing jar, topping it with a bow of green ribbon. Placed in the centre of a table, this can easily become a conversation piece. Another good idea with bottles is to fill them with coloured water ; a few drops of red, blue or green ink will give the desired effect. A frill or a doily, fixed to the top of such a bottle, in the centre of which a cluster of short-stemmed flowers is placed, can prove a very effective top-knot.

You may wish to make candles your party accent, in which case see that no other illumination is used, so that your candle-light will be remembered. Try those long burning candles placed inside large brandy glasses ; fish bowls or gas globes are equally effective. They present quite a change, especially if a number of coloured glass marbles are thrown into the bottom of the glass surrounding the candle. Then there are those big, multi-coloured, twisted candles that have such an appeal for country homes. I have fixed one or more of these to the base of a dish with a wedge of Plasticine, then surrounded the candle with colourful fruit ; or greenery may be inserted into the Plasticine.

In many of the good stores you can find candles in all shapes and colours, some bearing the figures ' 21 ' suitable for 21st birthday celebrations ; others, featuring sprigs of heather and horseshoes, are ideal for wedding candelabra. In fact, if candle-light appeals to you there is no end to the variations you can apply. You can use them to accentuate a colour scheme, whether harmonious or contrasting—lime-green candles on a cinnamon-brown cloth could be a talking point, just as pale pink or mauve candles on a dove-grey or pink organdie cloth would produce a colour harmony for an intimate occasion.

● *A tall ' Marigold tree ' built up on a dowel stick is*
most effective at the top of a staircase or,
like this one, on a buffet table where
it can be seen above the heads of standing guests.

● *Even a few flowers can attract attention if*
the colour scheme is well thought out.
These peach-coloured pom-pom Dahlias,
placed on a pin-holder in a dish standing on
a brown wooden platter, are
surrounded by lime-green coloured fruit.

● *A dry arrangement of Old Man's Beard, Teazles and coloured berries grouped behind a piece of wood on a tray makes an interesting feature for an informal country party in the autumn.*

• Though inexpensive, the pale green of wild Spurge gives a
distinctive note when arranged in a white alabaster chalice,
with grapes providing weight and interest in the centre.

• An interesting and unusual plant material in an unusual container—a green
glass water bottle holds green tassels of Amaranthus caudatus,
with Funkia leaves providing change of textural form.
Colour interest is given by the centrally placed red Rowan berries.

● *Make a talking point with unusual flowers.*
Here stems of coral-coloured Echiveria
are held in wire-netting
and backed by dried
sea fern in a brown mottled shell.

● *This engagement-party buffet table emphasizes the favourite colour of the bride-to-be*
with an arrangement of pale pink Gladioli and Antirrhinums
and deep pink Carnations, all held on a pin-holder and crumpled wire-netting
in a silver compotier.   The table is covered with pale pink
nylon over a white sheet draped with deep pink nylon entwined with pearls.

● *Pale yellow Heathcoat nylon draped with lime-green adorns this buffet table for a party at which Mimosa is the dominating floral motif.*

● *Height and depth of interest are important when ' dressing up ' a piece*
of sculpture.   This turquoise-green pottery head is
given height by Cycas leaves ; pink and cerise
Rhododendrons are tucked into a dish of water at the back
to complete an arrangement with a difference.

● *A design with a*
  difference—
  a glass jar filled
  with bright red
  Rowan berries.
  Height and form
  contrast are
  provided by
  Bulrushes and
  green
  Funkia leaves.

98

● *A basket of Lilac on an
entrance hall table
offers a delightful
welcome to May visitors.*

● An amusing ' party piece ' for autumn.
   The balances of a pair of grocer's
   brass scales hold sprays of
   berried Berberis,
   greenery and fruit.
   Grapes were added for extra effect.

● Here is a different touch for a door or
   wall decoration.   Green apples are
   pierced in a pattern with beaded pins,
   and tied with silver strings
   gathered into a bow of ribbon.

● *A design to provide colour and interest on a*
side table.   Striped Amaryllis flowers
in tubes of water are tucked between
pineapples, grapes, peaches and bananas
on a large pewter server.

● *Another version of the ' tree ' theme.*
Three gilded grapefruit of varying
sizes are built up on a knitting
needle held in a gilded goblet.

Have you ever made Flower Trees? These can give an interesting and novel note to a dining or luncheon table. Screw a tin to the top of a dowel-stick, then fix the stick into a flower pot with the aid of Plasticine and stones, afterwards filling the tin with a mass of flowers of one type or colour. I once painted some flower pots turquoise-blue, using scarlet Carnations in the tin. On another occasion I made the trees much bigger; standing in tubs, the 'trunks' three feet high, and massed above with the annual Camellia flowering Godetia (grown easily from seed in two months), these trees made an effective decoration for a summer dance in a marquee. They are ideal if placed each side of the doorway on party nights and are also excellent for verandas and the tops of stairways.

Another novel decorative idea is to dress up your ornaments with flowers. Cluster them behind a piece of sculpture, a bronze or china figurine. Try making a 'scene' or a 'still-life' picture, adding fruit and accessories.

I recall the delight I experienced when for the first time—and it is always the first time you make a design which gives the greatest pleasure—I made a garland for a stairway. Starting at the top, the ribbon was looped here and there and finished at the bottom with a huge bunch of ribbon placed on top of the banister scroll. Into this a few Carnations were inserted, but the mass of shining ribbon caught the eye. For this idea silk-sheen ribbon, which is inexpensive, and remains stiff, can be obtained from most florists and some stores.

I enjoy the fun of trying something new. To me, making a new flower style is a challenge, and I am always at my best when up against it. In fact I become much more in a party mood if I can sense the exhilaration of adding the last decorative touch, almost with verve, just as the guests are arriving.

Once, when needing extra colour in the hall, I hung up an old birdcage, previously painted white, filled with bright red Geraniums. Any type of colourful flower can be used in such a cage, carefully arranged to hide the water-filled container ; the effect is most intriguing. Just as interesting is the use of wood combined with flowers. A twisted shape of tree wood, perhaps scraped free of bark, then polished or sand-blasted, gives textural feeling to many designs; in fact some pieces of wood picked up in the fields or the countryside, or the dead root ends of a felled tree, appear almost as pieces of wooden sculpture and need only a few flowers added for a highlight.

You might try using as a flower container an item which is not normally associated with flowers—for instance, a shopping basket filled with potted plants. Pile a large bowl with green apples, inserting wild Daisies here and there between the fruit ; the Daisies will not die if you put a dish of water covered with wire-netting (on which the fruit will rest) in the base of the bowl. Cabbage leaves can be combined with oranges and lemons in a large wooden salad bowl, or wheat and Dahlias in a copper kettle.

A grouping of gourds is always interesting, especially to those who do not grow them. They can be left in their natural state, or coloured or varnished. Gourds come in various and curious shapes and can easily be grown from seed sown in April or May ; if left on the vine until late summer, they can be picked when hard and will last all winter.

To obtain a strikingly 'different' effect, introduce some unusual flowers at your party. The colourful, wax-like Anthuriums, though appearing expensive, will last for weeks and a few of these exotic blooms will create a big stir if arranged angularly. Similarly, orange-coloured Clivias, usually in the shops in spring, are very long lasting, and they are dramatic in effect when arranged with sculptured wood and ornaments. Another expensive though very long-lasting bloom is the *Strelitzia reginae* (Bird of Paradise). This exotic-looking flower always creates great interest and either evokes tales from those guests who have seen them growing in tropical countries, or draws forth questions as to their name and how they are grown. They certainly make an impact and I would rather have a few of these on certain occasions than a mass of accepted seasonal flowers. There is a party place for them, and the occasion has to be well chosen.

All flower arrangement and decoration is expressive, so if you are not easily led into trying new decorative ideas which you may think are bizarre or even ridiculous, I do advise you to stick to your own ideas of arranging beautiful flowers. You may be an ardent and knowledgeable gardener, who enjoys displaying the results of your labour in the garden, in which case nothing could be better at *your* party than for you to show your flowers in a manner which is expressive of yourself and your background. Such displays will draw the admiration from others with similar tastes.

I have seen and enjoyed some of the most beautiful green and white arrangements, in which all manner of different foliages were introduced, to be followed in another setting with a view of six red Cannas protruding from a tall black cylinder; and the more I travel around, not only in my own but in other countries as well, the more I realise what vast scope there is for satisfying all tastes with the tremendous choice we have in plant material.

There is room for all styles and reasons for all of them, so in closing this chapter on ideas I would stress that in my experience the greatest value in flower arranging comes from the development of your own expression. I always try to persuade beginners in this art to try anything and not be intimidated by what 'this' or 'that' one says. Enjoying doing it is what counts, and if you put up a decoration of sedums in a pile of sea shells and tell your guests you did it because it reminded you of your summer holiday, then you are having fun.

The ideas I have mentioned are just a few intended to stimulate your own. Do remember to buy or pick your flowers the day before your party and to re-cut the stems, leaving them in deep water in a cool dark place for some hours or overnight until needed, and to submerge all foliage for hours before using it in order to make it turgid and strong.

Christmas

Christmas

THERE is no doubt about it, Christmas is the most exciting and important time of the year. Most of us love coping with the many necessary preparations for this festival—making puddings and mincemeat, shopping for attractive cards and presents and—best fun of all—decorating our homes. And what a chance Christmas gives us to conjure up all our ingenuity in this direction : the scope is almost limitless.

I like to take advantage of all the varied greenery available, dressing it up with ribbons, baubles, cones and glitter. Cut branches of fir, if stood in a painted tin full of earth, will make a good substitute for a Christmas tree ; they last well, too, for fir needles do not easily drop. If your Christmas tree is bought several days beforehand, it can be kept fresh by standing it in a bucket of water to which a proprietary brand of fertiliser has been added. When decorating a room or a hall for a party, it would be well to treat the tree and any other greenery with a fire-resistant solution consisting of a pound of ammonium sulphate (obtainable from the chemist) to two gallons of water. Spread newspapers on the ground or floor and spray the solution on to your tree and green foliage, allowing it to dry before placing it in position.

Holly, beautiful and festive in appearance, loses its leaves quite quickly in heated rooms, but it will last longer if the stems, especially at the leaf joints, are brushed over with thin glue or clear varnish. Another effective treatment is to spray the leaves and stems with hair lacquer to hold them firmly in place.

For white decorations, using large leafless branches, seed heads, barley, wheat, pine or yew, you will need a pail or bath of oil-based white distemper. Swish all the material through this solution and hang the items upside down to drip and dry. Silver or gold glass glitter can be sprinkled on just before the distemper is dry or, if the material has been prepared well in advance, it can be brushed over on the day of assembly with thin glue and the glitter sprinkled on from a flour sieve.

White liquid shoe-polish or flat white paint is excellent for covering individual leaves such as Magnolia, Laurel, Rhododendron and Cycas, and it is useful for cones and bark when you want them just flicked with white on the edges. For a heavy snow effect on the tree, whisk up a bowl of concentrated soap-flakes and flick the foam on to the branches, where it will settle like bubbly snow and stay firm.

Children are thrilled to help at Christmas time by collecting cones, pine, nuts and other decorations. They may indeed enjoy an afternoon painting or gilding what they have collected, leaving the items ready to be assembled by grown-ups. When I was a child—the eldest of seven—we always enjoyed making animals and " Wise men " from Plasticine for a manger scene, which we constructed each year to go on a chest of drawers standing on a landing of my family home. I am sure that this simple representation of the Christ Child's crib stressed the true significance of the occasion.

Another of my childhood memories when Christmas was spent in the country is of the paper chase always organised on Boxing Day, to which our young friends were invited. I have no doubt that it was arranged to get us out into the fresh air, but we never failed to enjoy it, returning home in the dusk with enthusiasm for the tea party which followed.

You might change the decorative accent of your party during the Christmas period to suit the occasion. At a children's party the emphasis could be placed on Father Christmas, his reindeer and sleigh, the latter filled with small gifts. A Punch and Judy show always delights children, and coloured balloons which can be taken home afterwards are a good idea. A conjuror, or games of magic, can be introduced at parties for older children, for they love testing their own powers of observation. Fancy Dress parties are eagerly anticipated, the preparation being half the fun. If a spare room is available, it could be arranged to represent the background of a pantomime, a fairy story, or a book title, the young guests being asked to come dressed as the characters concerned. Imagine the fun arising out of a background design of Aladdin's Cave ! Small presents could even be made to appear as if by magic at the rubbing of a lamp or lantern.

Family dinner parties at Christmas time are happy and intimate gatherings and although drinks and greetings will be exchanged as visiting members arrive, one of the main attractions will be the table. Take great thought for your centrepiece, which could be a tall candelabrum holding red candles and decorated with ribbon and holly, or a low design of Christmas Roses and variegated holly, flanked on each side with a single yellow candle in a silver candlestick. Colours will of course depend on your general scheme of decoration, your table mats or cloth, china, etc. Bon-bons add a touch of gaiety, and individual snow scenes as place-name settings are original. These may be made from plaster powder mixed with water to a thick paste and poured into the lids of cocoa tins. Sprigs of greenery and small Christmas ornaments should then be stuck into position before the plaster sets firm, the name cards being added at the last minute. See that there are plenty of ash trays, matches, condiment sets

109

and other ancillary items on the table so that your guests do not have to slow down conversation by fidgeting for something they want.

Families reunited at Christmas love reminiscing. Plenty of good food and drink, a blazing fire and comfortable chairs all help to create the intimate atmosphere in which family tales are retold and ' the ghost of Christmas past ' is raised again. Such occasions may be enlivened by the showing of films or coloured slides of various branches of the family on holiday. For those who can summon up the energy, charades or single mime acts of ' What am I ? ' are invariably popular, and so are some writing games.

I'm sure that you will find that your guests will appreciate your thoughtfulness in providing an atmosphere of good cheer that they would not have thought of themselves, and a particularly colourful setting can be provided by burning on the fire pine cones that flare with a brilliant orange flame. The treatment of the cones is simple. First dry well in the oven, then brush over with glue and sprinkle, before the glue has dried, with chemist's calcium chloride.

An evening buffet party is an excellent way of entertaining a dozen or more friends and gives a hostess a splendid opportunity of using her ingenuity. Try covering one or more long trestle tables with white cloths over which strips of wide red ribbon are laid lengthways and crosswise, as though wrapping a parcel. At the cross sections arrange sprigs of yew and ribbon bows, and to accentuate the colour scheme place candles in tall bottles filled with red-coloured water at intervals along the length of the table. A few drops of red ink will colour the water.

Plenty of cold meat dishes should be offered, with chicken, ham and turkey vol-au-vents as an alternative. Small cooked chipolatas rolled in a slice of ham or turkey and speared with a toothpick are easy to handle, while chopped chicken with cold rice, peas and chopped celery mixed with mayonnaise makes a delicious dish. Plenty of French bread, butter, paper napkins, plates and utensils should be available, and, as single plates are not easy to handle with a glass in the other hand, as much sitting-down room as possible should be provided for your guests. Card tables can be covered to the same plan as the large tables, or the motif can be reversed, with white ribbon on red paper cloths, and a candle in a bottle as centrepiece. Candles in wine or beer bottles are always effective. Nuts and fruit can be placed on the small tables, although mince pies, which are essential for a Christmas party, should go at one end of a large serving table with the coffee. The other end of your table will probably be reserved for the punch bowl.

Dancing is always welcomed at Christmas parties, so, if there is room, be

● *In the absence of a real tree, this sophisticated-looking substitute can be made from aluminium wire strips (which can be bought by the yard) built up on a dowel stick.   The Santa Claus is made from stiff red paper and cotton wool.*

● *This table fantasia is a variation on the tree motif.   Three frills of spotted net*
are held on a knitting needle fixed with Plasticine into a glass goblet,
which is then filled with shredded Cellophane.
Use several along the length of the table.
The place settings of silver ribbon and diamanté pick up the theme.

● *Flowers and fruit combine admirably in this party arrangement for a sideboard.
The vase is filled with wire-netting over a pin-holder which holds
the tall Gladioli, Carnations and greenery in position. The fruit,
grouped on the mound of netting, is held firmly in place with toothpicks.*

● *A delightful setting for a small family Christmas dinner party. For the centre-piece a silver candlestick is placed in an entrée dish and surrounded by crumpled wire-netting holding long sprays of Yew, shorter stems of berried Holly and red Carnations. Crackers, balloons (some covered with coloured hair-nets) and snowmen holding place cards add festive gaiety.*

● *Another tree, perhaps to decorate a side table from which a welcoming drink is served. Three frills of pleated gold paper held with rings of Plasticine to a dowel stick and topped with a bauble. More frills can be opened flat and hung round the room.*

● *A Christmas Carol scene built on an old tin tray. Plaster filler powder mixed with water makes the snow, on which the bare branch, greenery, cones and berries are held by a pin-holder. The choir boys, whose heads can be made from ping-pong balls or Plasticine, stand in front of a toy lamp-post.*

● *This symphony in silver and white makes perfect a centre-piece for Weidart's glass tableware.*
Silver diamanté glittered leaves, silver tulle ribbon
and baubles are pressed into Plasticine round a candle on a silver cakeboard base.

● *A hanging decoration for the chimney-piece.*
The items are held together with
wire and fixed in place with Sellotape.

● *One of a group of individual Christmas party tables, with a
colour scheme of red and gold.   Red twill, fixed
with bunches of greenery and red berries, drapes the white
tablecloth ; gilded Magnolia Grandiflora leaves,
inserted into Plasticine and finished with red glass baubles,
surround the base of the candelabrum with its bright red candles.*

● *This arrangement is ideal for a long table. ' Skeleton' leaves, ribbon bows*
and silver and pearl baubles, inserted into Plasticine
on a cakestand, form the centre-piece of the design, which is
flanked by bottles filled with green-coloured water decorated with ribbon,
glittered wheat ears and beads. The edges of the candles are glittered.

● *Greet your guests with claret cup and a gay hall*
table arrangement on Christmas morning.
The tall candelabrum is decorated
with sprays of green Fir, cones and
red ribbon, all held on a ring of Plasticine.

● *Lemons, green apples and oranges on a tiered*
  white pottery cake stand, topped with
  a flower-filled vase, make a
  colourful decoration for a buffet or side table.

● *An unusual and striking decoration using only candles and greenery. Tall*
white candles are pressed into blocks of Florapak (or block salt),
which also hold the greenery. Small angel candles placed
in procession complete the scene, built up on a large silver cakeboard base.

Sprigs of Yew, Holly and berries
spray out from a
cupholder on a candlestick
with a white candle and Christmas
bells, in this design for
the punch bowl and titbit table.

● *A cheerful pedestal design to greet your guests. Cycas leaves,
whitened with flat white paint and sprinkled down the
centre with glitter before the paint dries, are
arranged in wire in a triangular pattern; bows of
red ribbon, cones and baubles are added in the centre.*

● One for the door—a candystick
cut from stiff white art board
twisted with red gummed
wrapper ribbon.
Greenery, ribbon, bows and
cones are held on with wire.

● A stairway or hall decoration
made by fixing a long-burning
candle with Plasticine into
the base of a wire plant-holder.
Insert Holly and Yew into
the Plasticine and finish with
a bow of bright red ribbon.

● *Yew forms the background for this design for a door, with whitened cones tied together with red ribbon* (see p. 135).

● *Another gay door decoration where sprays of Juniper form the outline, with Rhododendron leaves, cones, red ribbon and berries added in the centre. The material is inserted into half a potato* (see p. 132).

125

• *Variations on the cone theme. These are made from half circles of silver, gold or coloured paper, and can represent trees or angels, or whatever your ingenuity suggests. Smaller ones are useful for individual place settings.*

• *Star-studded wrapping paper twisted into a cornucopia tied with red ribbon bows and filled with sprays of Yew to which are wired masses of multicoloured glass baubles.*

• *A good idea for a family table setting is to lay strips of red ribbon down the length and breadth of the white cloth to give the impression of a parcel wrapping. Bows of ribbon with green pine are pinned on at the cross-sections and red candles and glassware complete the theme.*

● *Leaves, apples and Fir cones wired*
on to a base of Cupressus
add a festive look
to Christmas table settings.
(For how to do it, see p. 135.)

● *Fresh Pine sprays,*
cones, Rhododendron leaves and
Cotoneaster berries held in
a ring of Plasticine and grouped
on a rectangular base
for the corner of a
chimney-piece.
Height is given by the
candle ; a bow of red ribbon
hangs over the
edge of the shelf.

● *Sugar frosting gives a festive*
sparkle to fruit.
Both the designs, in silver
containers, shown on this page
combine red apples with
white grapes, to which Holly
and Wheat ears are added.

● *Conical designs are particularly suitable for small rooms.*
This tree of Holly leaves and berries is built up on wire-netting in
a gilt-wood container. (See p. 138 for how to do it.)

● *Greenery, whitened*
leaves, ribbon
and baubles
attached with wire to the
top of a ribbon-covered
cardboard ring make
this hanging ornament.

● *A green-and-white*
arrangement which
will combine with
any colour scheme
—white candles,
Christmas Roses
and Pine sprays,
held on a pin-holder
in a shallow green
pottery dish.

prepared to roll back your carpet. It is not very expensive to hire a three-piece band or a guitarist; or it is always possible to dance to long-playing records or a tape recorder.

It is a good idea to make card games available to those who do not dance, while recording and listening to one's own voice on a tape recorder is another good party piece which never fails to interest and astonish guests. Hot soup, hot wine or whisky punches (see p. 10) can be served when your guests are ready to go home.

But it is impossible to generalise about Christmas parties because the settings, circumstances and reasons for the gatherings differ so much. The formal dinner party, the table set with choice glassware, silver and a glittering centre-piece, should be reserved for a few special friends, for unless plenty of domestic help is available, the serving of a well-chosen menu can be a trial. For such a party a small gift in gay wrapping can mark each place-setting and tinsel ribbon posies placed here and there on the table can later be transferred to the ladies' hair or dresses.

Christmas party settings call for special decorations. I have no doubt that each should be emphasised in one colour scheme or represented on one theme which is suitable to the background and occasion. For instance, a well-timbered, old country house would be suitably decorated with fresh plant material and berries set with logs and robins, pewter, brass and pottery being the correct accessories for holding flowers, fruit, nuts and sweets. Whereas silver ribbon, glass baubles and shining Christmas trees would prove the perfect complements to a sophisticated town drawing-room. We all have our pet theories and ideas for Christmas decoration and we can all be right. The ideas which I offer are intended only to stimulate your own.

I recall one occasion when I offered to help decorate a village hall. The high walls were completely bare, so from the picture rail we hung, at intervals, long strips of wide red ribbon. At the end of each of these strips we fixed a bunch of greenery and cones at about shoulder height. To avoid monotony we then covered rings made of wire (cardboard or embroidery rings would do) with ribbon, again adding sprigs of greenery and cones at the base of each ring. These were hung in between the long ribbon strips, but ended a little higher up. Cones can easily be fixed to all sorts of bases if they are given false stems by wiring them as illustrated on page 135.

Wall or hanging wall decorations can be made by inserting pieces of yew or holly or other greenery into a potato. First tie round the potato with string or ribbon, leaving sufficient ends for hanging, and then insert the short stems of greenery and berries at intervals so that the potato is completely covered. Add baubles for sparkle. I have found these decorations most effective when hung in front of drawn curtains. A ball of greenery looks wonderful with a background of red curtains, and a silvered ring against blue curtains. Yellow curtains as a background for a red-and-green decoration can be the high spot of any room.

The same potato base idea can be employed for door decorations, but only one side of the potato should be covered, the other being cut flat to allow it to hang flush with the door. The longest sprays of greenery should be inserted on the outside, the cones, larger leaves and ribbon being placed near the centre.

Another hanging idea suitable for a hall is to use a wire lampshade frame, painting it white, gold or silver. Fix strands of ribbon to both top and bottom, tying the lower ones together and adding a bunch of greenery so that it hangs down. The top strands are then knotted together in a manner which will allow the decoration to be hung.

Fresh plant material is always a welcome sight, especially on the Christmas table, so try using sprays of green yew or pine with Christmas Roses or red Carnations or Anemones. Colourful candles will add height to a grouping of short flowers. Fruit also adds a gay note to the table or sideboard. Pile into an enormous dish apples and oranges which have been flicked with egg white or boiled sugar-water and sprinkled with glitter, whole bunches of grapes dipped first in beaten egg and then in castor sugar, and add coloured baubles and gold-painted nuts. The result is astonishing.

Don't forget what a valuable aid Plasticine can be. Use it in a thick ring round the top of a bottle holding a candle, inserting sprays of greenery into the Plasticine, with the possible addition of a ribbon bow. Try pressing a candle into a thick ring of Plasticine and place the whole on a silvered cardboard cake-stand. An original scheme of decoration can then be completed by inserting sprays of whitened yew, leaves, baubles and ribbon low down into the Plasticine.

Glass or diamanté glitter, gold and silver paints, coloured and flock papers can all be obtained from Art Stores. Candles, brushed over with thin glue and rolled in glitter, can stand as sentinels and add sparkle to dark corners.

Where space is limited, decorations based on the shape of a cone are useful. They have the advantage of being easily made in any size and in a variety of coloured materials, giving the appearance of Christmas trees. Large green ones standing at each side of a doorway are most effective, while a number of smaller ones cut from silver wrapping paper and placed over wine glasses will give a gay touch if placed at intervals along the length of a festive table. To make these

133

cone-shaped trees you need a circle of paper, tarlatan or stiffened net. Cut the circle in half, and twist it round to form a conical shape, fixing it with Sellotape. The cone can then rest on a dowel-stick if you are making a large tree, or a knitting needle if your tree is small, and held in a tin, glass or flower pot according to size. Red art-paper cones, sprinkled with sequins and set in white flower-pots, are ideal for the ends of buffet tables, whereas smaller gold-paper ones, held in gold-painted tins and finished with ribbon, never fail to evoke comment.

Sequins remind me of one of the prettiest table decorations I have ever made. I covered the main cloth with tulle and lightly touched this here and there with thin glue, sprinkling sequins and glitter over it. The centrepiece was made from bows of tulle on wire stems, grouped with baubles. A frothy but altogether gay affair !

You cannot have failed to notice my particular liking for candle-light at Christmas time ; its soft glimmer seems to me to spread benediction. Whether I place a large candle inside a glass globe or witch bowl, standing it in a window with blinds undrawn, or light my dining table with candelabra, I am certain to find some method of introducing them into my decorative scheme. I like to use a candle even on a landing or in some quiet corner of the room ; wherever it is, it seems to give a message of peace and goodwill to all men at this hallowed time.

How to do it

● *These two photographs show how to*
prepare apples, leaves and
similar small items
so that they can be fixed on
to other material . . .
for instance, to a piece of rope
for a wall decoration
such as that on p. 71.
Florists' stub wires are first bent
into the shape of hairpins
which, when apples are being used,
are inserted down through the
top of the fruit
and the ends twisted to
make false stems.

● *For cones, the wire is wound*
carefully round the lower
scales before being twisted
into stems.   Firm hat wire can
also be used—and so,
of course, can hairpins !

135

● Here are some of the necessary containers and gadgets for the flower arranger. The tall cone, when held in a vase by crumpled wire-netting, makes it possible for a taller effect to be obtained in the centre when using medium-length flowers. The shell is filled with Mosette, a plastic-like foundation useful for dry material and small-stemmed flowers such as Freesias. Shallow dishes are ideal for modern or Japanese-styled designs and of course the 'Original' pin-holders are essential for most arrangements. The metal candle-cup flower holder (above cone, lower left) is for insertion in candlesticks and bottles.

● Short flowers with stems of the same length can be built up in tiers by putting one vase inside another, using crumpled wire-netting in the lower container. (See p. 23.)

● One way of making a Christmas
‘ tree ’ for the table.
First cover a dowel stick by
winding coloured passe-partout or
ribbon round it (or just paint it).
Then fix one end, with
Plasticine, into a flower pot
or similar container
and fill up the pot with sand
or small stones.
Press an apple onto the top of
the stick and insert into it
sprigs of greenery
in a symmetrical pattern.

● The finished tree. Baubles, small
cones and berries can be added
if they are not too heavy,
and the container may
be embellished with a bow
and Cellophane shavings.
The dowel stick will be held
more firmly in its pot if Plaster
of Paris is used instead
of Plasticine and stones.

137

● *This conically shaped ' tree ' is ideal for small rooms or where little space is available. Make a cone of wire-netting and fill it with sphagnum moss. Soak this thoroughly in water and press the lower part well into the container.*

● *Wire short twigs, leaves of holly and berries and insert these into the mossy cone until it is completely covered. Reserve the largest leaves for spreading out lower down over the rim of the container.*

Care of Cut Flowers

NOTHING is more maddening than to have spent money, time and skill in arranging flowers for a special event, only to find them drooping a few hours later.

Of course many methods have been expounded for lengthening the life of cut flowers, each dealing expertly with one particular flower ; but if we tried to carry out all of this advice we should spend the best part of the day wondering which flower to put with which and whether to cut, burn, strip or dip the stem ends in this, that or the other.

I will try to reduce the mass of complex information on this subject, so that a busy hostess can arrive at a fairly simple answer to suit her particular needs. There are always exceptions to general rules ; for instance, the most useful calculations can be upset by climatic conditions or the time of picking the flowers. The following generalisations, however, have worked and proved very valuable to me.

Always buy or pick your flowers the day before the party.

If picking from the garden, leave this operation until the evening.

Strip off lower leaves, recut *the stem ends and leave in deep water in a dark place until required. This treatment will harden them and fully charge the stems with water.*

Follow the same method, but leave in full light those blooms which are not fully opened, such as tightly budded Paeonies, Gladioli, Roses and Anemones.

All woody-stemmed flowers, such as Lilac, Viburnums, Chrysanthemums, Roses and other flowering shrubs should have some leaves removed, stem ends split and be placed in deep water until required.

Leaves and sprays of greenery should be submerged in water for hours before being used to make them turgid and strong. In spring and early summer it is best to place such young leaves in a bath of water all night before the party.

Tulips will always turn and twist towards the light. Wrap them up to their heads in newspaper and leave in deep water overnight before using. They should then have taken their stand.

If you have the time certain flowers such as Delphiniums and Lupins will benefit by having their hollow stems filled with water after cutting, with cotton wool inserted afterwards as a plug. Do this before leaving them in deep water overnight to be conditioned.

If flowers for a party arrive rather wilted, recut the stem ends and place in hot water. The exception would be soft-stemmed flowers such as Tulips which must not be given this treatment.

For parties, buy unusual flowers such as Strelitzia Reginae, Anthuriums, Clivias or Orchids which you know will last ; or choose those which are in season.

It is inadvisable to buy Sweet Peas in January. They will not last in a hot room because they have been artificially forced for the market. Far better to leave these sweet-smelling flowers until the summer when they will share their beauty and scent with you for many days.

Always have water—warm water is best—in the vase before arranging your flowers ; this avoids the drying of the stem ends.

There is now a very good powder on the market named ' Chrysal ' which helps flowers last longer. Being a plant nutrient, it adds days to the life of cut flowers and is also excellent for leaves.

The leaves of many flowers foul the water if left on the stem ; in particular it is wise to remove the leaves of Stocks, Antirrhinums, Clarkias, Godetias. Often the addition of leaves of another kind give a change of form in the design.

Do not overlook the attraction of an all-foliage arrangement, which lasts well if the leaves are soaked in water overnight. A few flowers can be added if needed.

A tablet of charcoal in the water of a vase will keep the contents pure. Top up with water each day.

Get to know your flowers and I am certain that knowledge and practice combined with (1) recutting the stem ends, (2) giving an overnight's deep drinking and (3) placing water in the container first will prolong the freshness and life of your party flowers.

Recipes

The best parties must have eats and drinks as well as flowers. I have tried with success all the following recipes and hope they will help your entertaining and add to your prestige as a hostess !